The Missions of California

Mission
San Juan Capistrano

Kathleen J. Edgar and Susan E. Edgar

The Rosen Publishing Group's
PowerKids Press™
New York

Published in 2000, 2002 by The Rosen Publishing Group, Inc.
29 East 21st Street, New York, NY 10010

Revised Edition 2002

Book Design: Danielle Primiceri

Photo Credits and Illustration Credits: pp. 1, 4, 6, 27, 30, 41 © SuperStock; p.5 © Stock Montage; pp. 7, 45 © CORBIS-Bettman; p. 9 © CORBIS/Paul A. Sonders; pp. 10, 12, 21, 27 © Eda Rogers; p. 11 © Michael K. Ward; pp. 13, 16, 17, 20, 36, 38; p. 14 © Department of Special Collections, University of Southern California Library; p. 15 © CORBIS/Kevin R. Morris; pp. 18, 19, 29, 31, 33, 46, 47, 48 © Christina Taccone; pp. 22, 28, 43 © The Bancroft Library; pp. 32 (all), 49, 51 © Shirley Jordan; pp. 35, 40, 44, 50, © North Wind Picture Archive; p. 49 © Varnel Jordan; pp. 52, 57 © Christine Innamorato.

Editorial Consultant Coordinator: Karen Fontanetta, M.A., Curator, Mission San Miguel Arcángel
Editorial Consultant: Gerald J. Miller, Administrator, Old Mission San Juan Capistrano
Historical Photo Consultants: Thomas L. Davis, M.Div., M.A., Michael K. Ward, M.A.

Edgar, Kathleen J.
    Mission San Juan Capistrano / by Kathleen J. Edgar and Susan E. Edgar.
      p. cm. — (Missions of California)
Includes index.
ISBN 0-8239-5889-2
1. Mission San Juan Capistrano—History Juvenile literature. 2. Spanish mission building—California, San Juan Capistrano Region—History Juvenile literature. 3. Franciscans—California—San Juan Capistrano Region—History Juvenile literature. 4. Juaneño Indians—Missions—California—San Juan Capistrano Region—History Juvenile literature. 5. California—History—To 1846 Juvenile literature. I. Edgar, Susan E. II. Title. III. Series.
F869.S395 E34 1999
                                                   99-31530
                                                    CIP

Contents

The Spanish Arrive in Alta California

In the San Juan Valley, near the Pacific Ocean, lies the quaint city of San Juan Capistrano. In the center of the city is a dust-colored brick wall that runs the length of a city block. Imposing and fortresslike, this wall shields what's behind it from the curious eyes of passersby. As they pass through the front gate, though, the sights seem uncontainable.

Inside the compound, there seems to be a small town plaza with a fountain in the center. Around the grounds are workshops and soldiers' barracks topped with rust-colored tiles. Trees and cacti grow abundantly. Swallows' mud-nests are tucked under the roof eaves, built by the thousands of swallows that live at the mission from March to October each year.

This little town within the city is the restored mission complex of the Mission San Juan Capistrano, which was the 7th of 21 missions founded by the Spanish between 1769 and 1823 in California. The center shows visitors what life was like for the Spanish missionaries and soldiers and the American Indians who lived in the area during the late eighteenth and early nineteenth centuries.

Near the center of the mission complex is a cone-shaped structure made of reeds lashed together. This is what the homes of the native people of the area, the Acágchemem Indians, looked like several hundred years ago. Off in the distance are the remains of a huge stone church, built by the Spanish and the Indians, that once stood on the mission grounds. The elaborate church was destroyed during an earthquake in 1812.

Mission San Juan Capistrano is a window to the past. It reminds us of what life was like more than 200 years ago.

Spanish Interest in Alta California

The Spanish became interested in the land we now call California after Christopher Columbus discovered the New World (North America, South America, and Central America) in 1492. Many countries wanted to send explorers to these new lands. The king of Spain sent men to the New World to see what riches it offered, hoping to find gold and spices.

▲

Christopher Columbus reached America in 1492.

Some of the Spanish also wanted to claim the New World for religious reasons. The Franciscans were one religious group that wanted to share their religion with the American Indians of the New World. The Spanish were Catholics and believed in the teachings of Jesus Christ and the Bible. They believed that only Christians had peace after they died. They wanted to convert the Indians to Catholicism to save their souls.

In 1542, the Spanish sent Juan Rodríguez Cabrillo to the Californias by ship. In those days, the term "Californias" was used to describe the area of land that includes today's state of California and the Baja Peninsula of Mexico. The southern portion of the Californias was named Baja, or lower, California, while the northern portion was called Alta, or upper, California.

Cabrillo explored the Alta California coast and discovered what would later be called San Diego Bay. During their visit, Cabrillo's party

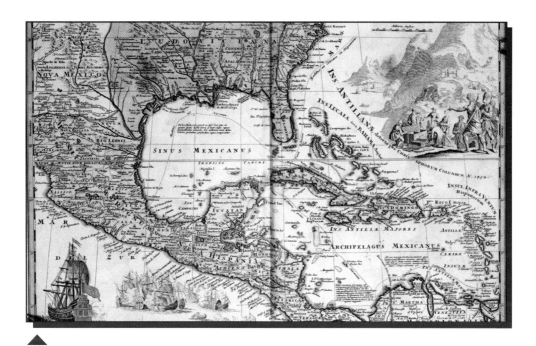

A map of New Spain.

came in contact with the American Indians already living on this land. Cabrillo described these people as friendly and peaceful. The Spanish crew traded things like cloth and beads with the Indians for berries, seeds, and other foods.

The Spanish began settling Alta California in 1769. They feared that settlers from Russia and England would move in if they did not establish themselves there. The Spanish sent five expeditions of soldiers, missionaries, and Indians who had already been converted in New Spain (today's Mexico) into Alta California. Their goal was to construct a chain of missions, or religious settlements, along the Pacific coastline.

The expeditions left New Spain under the command of Captain

Gaspár de Portolá. He was accompanied by the religious leader Fray Junípero Serra. Fray is the Spanish word for friar. Fray Serra, who was selected by the Roman Catholic Church to become the mission president of Alta California, joined Portolá's group. Two expeditions traveled the dusty, rocky route over land, and three ships sailed the rough waters of the Pacific Ocean. One ship got lost at sea. The groups met at San Diego. Many men got sick or died on the way. Only about half of the 219 men who began the journey made it to Alta California.

While Portolá went off in search of the area an earlier expedition had chosen to be the site of the second mission, Fray Serra and other men began building Mission San Diego de Alcalá.

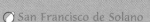

○ San Francisco de Solano
○ San Rafael Arcángel
○ San Francisco de Asís
  ○ San José

    ○ Santa Clara de Asís
○ Santa Cruz
  ○ San Juan Bautista
○ **San Carlos Borromeo del Río Carmelo**
  ○ Nuestra Señora de la Soledad

○ **San Antonio de Padua**
    ○ San Miguel Arcángel

○ **San Luis Obispo de Tolosa**

  ○ La Purísima Concepción
  ○ Santa Inés
    ○ Santa Bárbara
      ○ San Buenaventura

      ○ San Fernando Rey de España
      ○ **San Gabriel Arcángel**

        ○ San Juan Capistrano

        ○ San Luis Rey de Francia

        ○ San Diego de Alcalá

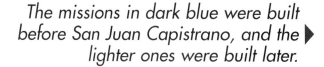

The missions in dark blue were built before San Juan Capistrano, and the ▶ lighter ones were built later.

Fray Juan Crespí, a former student of Fray Serra's, accompanied Portolá on the journey north.

On July 22, 1769, Crespí wrote in his diary about seeing Indians as they passed through the area where San Juan Capistrano would be founded. He noted that there were many trees and meadowlands, a valley, and plenty of water. The group named this lush spot Santa Maria Magdalena. Later, they also called it Wildfire Hollow because a brush fire had swept through the area. Crespí wrote that a boy and an infant had been burned in the fire. He baptized them on the spot because the children were near death. After the discovery of this land, seven years passed before Mission San Juan Capistrano was founded.

The Swallows of Capistrano

One of the unique features of Mission San Juan Capistrano are the thousands of cliff swallows that build their nests among the ruins each year. The small birds arrive each March to build their nests. In October they fly to South America, traveling nearly 6,000 miles (9,656 kilometers), only to return again in the spring.

The cliff swallows make their nests out of balls of mud, which they scoop up with their beaks. When finished, the nests resemble a jug or vase. Visitors to the mission can see the mud nests hanging under the roofs of the mission buildings.

The Acágchemem Indians

The Indians who lived in the area where Mission San Juan Capistrano would later be founded were mainly from the Acágchemem tribe or group. When the Spanish arrived, they called these Indians Juaneño. The Acágchemem did not have a written history, but historians have been able to piece together information about the way they lived before the Spanish came through artifacts (like tools, clothing, baskets, bowls, and weapons) and stories the Acágchemem have passed down from generation to generation.

▲

This is an Acágchemem home made of tule reeds.

Like many of the American Indian tribes in Alta California, the Acágchemem lived in small villages, most of which were near a source of water. The Acágchemem villages were built around a central plaza. They made their homes in a cone shape by using a wooden form and lashing reeds and brush on top of it. The brush was attached in layers, like shingles on a house, to keep the inside dry. Their homes were called *kiitcas*.

The Acágchemem life was based on the natural world. Their religion, clothing, weapons, food, and homes were all dependent upon nature. Fending for themselves was essential to their survival, so they learned early to get everything they needed from their environment.

The Acágchemem men and women worked together to make sure their tribe had enough food and other resources. The men were responsible for

The life of an Acágchemem was based on the natural world. ▶

10

Acágchemem were taught how to fish with nets and spears.

hunting and fishing. Wearing little or no clothing during the summer months, they snared or trapped birds, squirrels, rabbits, mice, quail, and ducks. To trap an animal, the hunters sometimes set fire to the brush to force the animal to run right into the trap. They also hunted deer and antelope. They fished, caught sharks, and searched for oysters and clams.

The men constructed their tools and weapons from natural resources, such as rocks, animal bones, shells, and sticks. They made arrowheads and spear tips out of rocks and a naturally occurring glass called obsidian, which is hard and cuts easily. The Acágchemem constructed bows from sturdy, flexible tree branches and bowstrings from vegetable stalks or animal sinew.

The women were often responsible for gathering food and taking care of the children. Wearing apronlike skirts made out of hides, grass, or bark, they searched for edible plants and insects. They gathered cattail seeds, rushes, yucca stalks, wild plums, currants, celery, berries, seaweed, roots, and acorns. They stored food in tightly woven baskets that they made out of reeds. They also constructed baskets for cooking, hauling water, and carrying their children.

One of the major sources of nutrition in the Acágchemems' diet was acorns. In the fall they gathered the nuts from the ground, or sometimes men and boys would climb the oak trees and shake or knock the acorns down with a stick. Once the acorns were collected, the women had to take special care in preparing them in order to remove a bitter acid that made them taste bad and could cause illness. After shelling the acorns, they crushed the nuts into flour. Then they cleaned the flour 10 times. Once the flour was clean, the women used it to make soups, cakes, and breads.

Most Acágchemem villages had a shaman, or medicine man, who used herbs and rituals to heal the sick. The Indians believed that shamans were able to communicate with spirits and were very important to the community. The canoebuilders and chiefs of each village were also significant and wore long robes made of elk hides. In addition to dealing with community issues, the chief served as the group's religious leader.

The Acágchemem religion was based on nature. All of the earth's creatures were significant and respected. The Acágchemem believed in many gods and spirits. Some of these beings brought good fortune and happiness, while others were responsible for bad situations. To please their gods, the Indians held many rituals and ceremonies, which included dancing and singing. They used these ceremonies to acknowledge deaths, weddings, births, new chiefs, war, hunting trips, and initiations into adulthood for boys and girls.

Though the Acágchemem clearly had a full life and culture, the Spanish were determined to have the Indians take on their lifestyle. The Acágchemems' lifestyle would be changed forever by the missionaries' arrival in 1776.

The Mission System

Before founding the missions in Alta California, the Spanish built similar religious settlements in New Spain. Spanish soldiers, missionaries, and settlers began missions in Central America, South America, and Baja California in the 1500s. They set up their government headquarters in Mexico City, which became the capital of New Spain.

Many Indians lived in New Spain. The Spanish built their missions near large Indian populations because they wanted to convert the Indians to Christianity and teach them Spanish practices. The Spanish thought they could help the Indians by teaching them European trades, religion, and the Spanish language.

The Indians lived much differently than the Spanish did, so the Spanish regarded the Indians as "savages." The Indians wore little or no clothing, while the Spanish men wore shirts and trousers and the Spanish women wore floor-length dresses. The Indians didn't attend schools, while many Spanish people did. The Spanish didn't recognize that the Indians' lifestyle was just as full and respectable as their own.

In New Spain, Franciscan friars taught the Indians about Spanish work methods. They showed the Indians how to care for livestock, plant and harvest crops, tool leather, work iron, make soap, and weave fabric for clothing. The friars also schooled the Indians in the Catholic religion and the Christian god.

▲

The Spanish brought cattle to Alta California.

◀ *The stone church at Mission San Juan Capistrano was the largest of all the mission churches in Alta California.*

The Indians were taught to use Spanish farming and irrigation methods.

Soldiers helped the friars build the settlements. They guarded the settlement from non-Spanish settlers or Indians who didn't want the Spanish on their land. They also built presidios, or military fortresses, to

16

keep the area safe from attack. There were four presidios in Alta California. They were spaced between the missions so the soldiers could ride to whatever mission needed help.

The missionaries who joined in this expansion followed the same basic procedures that were used to build the missions in New Spain. Once each mission was established, it was to be controlled by the Spanish for about 10 years. The Spanish estimated that this was enough time to convert the Indians to Christianity and teach them European trades. Then operation of the mission would be turned over to the Indians, who would become Spanish citizens. This process was called secularization. In this way, the Spanish gained control over new lands. In addition they would gain new citizens who had to pay taxes to Spain. Once a mission was secularized, the friars would travel to another area and help at other missions.

The friars converted the Indians to Catholicism.

17

Founders of
Mission San Juan Capistrano

Many men played important roles in establishing the mission system in Alta California. Among them were Fray Junípero Serra and Fray Fermín Francisco de Lasuén.

Fray Serra

Fray Serra was the president of the Alta California mission chain at the time of the founding of Mission San Juan Capistrano. He was born on November 24, 1713, in Majorca, Spain. Serra became a Franciscan in 1731. He taught philosophy for nine years, but believed so strongly in the Catholic faith that he became a missionary in order to teach others about it. He volunteered to go to New Spain to work at the missions and was eventually put in charge of five of them.

When he was 55, Serra was chosen by Roman Catholic Church officials to be the mission president of Alta California. His first task was to travel to that little-explored area and establish missions in two previously selected locations. This was a huge job for the small priest, who was often sick. While traveling to Alta California, Serra was suffering from a severe leg infection caused by an insect bite. He was very weak, but made the 750-mile (1,207 km) journey to the first mission site despite his illness.

▲

The statue of Fray Serra bears this plaque.

18

This statue of Fray Serra with Juan Evangelista, an Indian boy, stands at Mission San Juan Capistrano. ▶

▲

The Acágchemem helped build Mission San Juan Capistrano.

During his lifetime, Serra founded nine missions in Alta California. As president, he was always traveling to the missions to check on their progress, help the missionaries, and work with the Indians. He made his headquarters at Mission San Carlos Borromeo del Río Carmelo (the second mission founded) and tended to the missions for 15 years. Fray

20

Serra died on August 28, 1784, of general poor health. Today he is a candidate for sainthood, an honor given by the Catholic Church to someone who has shown an incredible devotion to God.

Fray Lasuén

Fray Lasuén was born on June 7, 1736, in Victoria, Spain. He became a missionary when he was a young man and arrived in New Spain in 1759 to spread his beliefs.

▲

Fray Lasuén worked with Fray Serra to establish the California missions.

Lasuén came to Alta California after Serra founded the first missions. He worked with Serra to establish others, including Mission San Juan Capistrano. After Serra's death, Lasuén was chosen to head the mission chain. During the time from 1785 to 1803, he founded nine missions and encouraged the friars to teach new work methods. He made many improvements in the areas of construction, planting and harvesting crops, and raising livestock.

Fray Lasuén died in 1803 at Mission San Carlos Borromeo del Río Carmelo, where he had also made his headquarters. He is buried in that mission's chapel alongside Fray Serra.

Establishing
Mission San Juan Capistrano

Founding the Mission

The first few missions established along the coast were far apart, so the Spanish began building more to close the distance between them. The San Juan Valley was the midpoint between Mission San Diego de Alcalá and Mission San Gabriel Arcángel. This valley was chosen as the site for the seventh mission in the chain: Mission San Juan Capistrano.

In October of 1775, Fray Lasuén was part of an expedition that traveled to the site where Mission San Juan Capistrano was to be founded. In his group were Fray Gregório Amúrrio, a small squad of soldiers from the presidio of Mission San Diego de Alcalá, and two Indian families originally from Baja California. They left Mission San Diego de Alcalá loaded with supplies for the new settlement, including cattle, grain, religious articles for the church, building materials, and tools. They arrived at the Indian village of Sajivit on October 30, and selected a site nearby for Mission San Juan Capistrano. Fray Lasuén blessed the land, and the members of the expedition erected a cross on the new mission site.

The group immediately began hauling timber to construct temporary shelters and a chapel. Eight days later, shocking news about Mission San Diego de Alcalá reached the party. On November 5, several hundred Indians had attacked the mission, stealing religious articles from the church and setting the mission buildings on fire. Several people were killed during the revolt, including the head missionary, Fray Luís Jaymé. The fighting stopped when the Spanish soldiers fired guns. Many of the Native Americans stayed on to help rebuild the mission.

◀ *This drawing shows Mission San Juan Capistrano many years after its founding.*

Fray Lasuén and his small group were all alone in the San Juan Valley, except for the Indians living in the Sajivit village. The Spanish didn't know how the local Acágchemem Indians would react to news of the revolt. The group didn't want to take any chances of being attacked, so they quickly buried the church bells they had brought with them, loaded up their belongings, and headed back to the presidio in San Diego to seek protection.

Tensions between the Spanish and the Indians around Mission San Diego de Alcalá quieted down after a while. The missionaries decided it was time to return to the San Juan Valley and start the mission all over again. This time Fray Serra led the expedition because Fray Lasuén was

Saint John of Capestrano

Mission San Juan Capistrano was named in honor of Saint John of Capestrano. He was born in 1385 in Capestrano, Italy. After becoming a priest in 1416, he was sent by Roman Catholic Church officials to preach throughout Europe. When he was 70, John led a Christian army to the Holy Lands (now the Middle East) in a war against the Turks. His army won the battle the following year. John caught a fever and died shortly thereafter. In 1724, John of Capestrano was named a saint. Sainthood is an honor given by the Catholic Church to someone who has shown an incredible devotion to God.

heading up construction efforts at another mission. The mission president was pleased with the site and called it a "place with abundant water, pasture, firewood and timber."

Serra found that the cross erected by Lasuén's group was still standing. They dug up the bells that had been buried and hung them from a tree. On November 1, 1776, Fray Serra conducted Mass, a Catholic religious service, and officially dedicated Mission San Juan Capistrano.

Building the Mission

Mission San Juan Capistrano took many years to build. After the first two years, there wasn't enough water in the area to drink or to keep the crops growing, so the mission was moved near an Acágchemem village where water was plentiful.

The mission complex was built to form a quadrangle, or a four-sided shape. It was surrounded by a wall that protected the mission like a fortress. The sides were not exact in length because the friars measured the length of each side by counting out paces, or number of steps, rather than using measuring instruments.

The friars and soldiers needed help building the mission. They attracted some of the local Acágchemem Indians by offering them food and trinkets such as glass beads. The Indians were also curious about the tools that the Spanish used, particularly axes made out of metal rather than stone. Eventually some of the Acágchemem began to help the missionaries.

In order to build permanent structures, the Spanish and the Acágchemem gathered the materials they needed from the surrounding area. They chopped down trees from the nearby forests of pine and oak, cut the trees into planks and building supports, and hauled them to

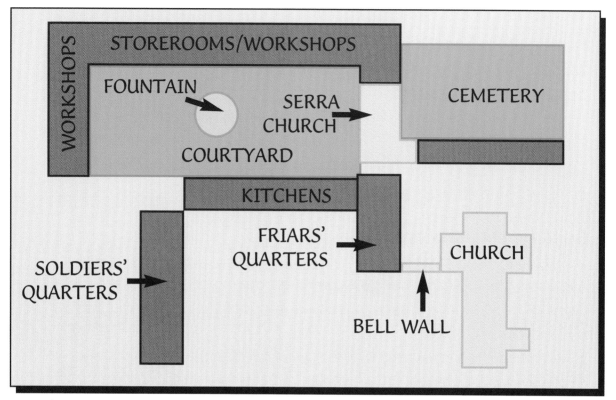

the construction site using *carretas,* or small wooden carts pulled by oxen or mules.

The missionaries showed the Acágchemem how to make adobe bricks for the walls. The women and children were taught to mix mud, water, and straw, stomping it together with their feet. When the mixture was ready, the workers packed it into wooden molds to make bricks. They placed the bricks in the sun to dry. The men placed the hardened bricks one on top of another in layers to make the walls, securing them with mud.

The workers made peaked roofs for the buildings using clay tiles, called *tejas.* Flat roofs were made with *terrado.* The workers made *terrado* roofs by laying brush and twigs on top of planks and then spreading adobe over it. The adobe would dry in the sun and make the *terrado* waterproof.

Over the next several years, the laborers built a church, living quarters for the missionaries, and dormitories for the Acágchemem who lived at the mission. They built storage rooms and granaries for the wheat and barley they planted and harvested in fields near the mission. They built weaving rooms, carpentry and blacksmithing shops, and soapmaking and candlemaking areas. They dug wells in the courtyard and constructed an irrigation

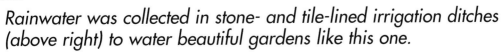

Rainwater was collected in stone- and tile-lined irrigation ditches (above right) to water beautiful gardens like this one.

27

▲

A painting of Mission San Juan Capistrano after the new stone church had been destroyed by an earthquake.

ditch from the Trabuco and San Juan Creeks to the mission, allowing water to flow into the crop fields.

By 1796, the chapel was too small to hold the number of neophytes living at the mission. Neophytes were Indians who had converted to Christianity. The friars decided to build a new church. After they started they realized they needed help. Isídro Aguilár, a master stonemason, was sent from New Spain to design a large stone church at Mission San Juan Capistrano. Inspired by the churches of Europe, Aguilár decided to build a church with a floorplan in the shape of a cross.

The church took nearly nine years to build. In 1800, a small earthquake shook the area and set construction back. Many of the pillars and support beams had to be replaced. When the church was finished in 1806, it measured 180 feet (55 m) long and 40 feet (12 m) wide. The arched ceiling was five stories high and had seven domes. The friars held a two-day festival and invited all the important leaders of Alta California to attend the first religious service held in the great church.

▲
Today Mission San Juan Capistrano has an elaborate church altar, which was made in Spain.

29

Daily Life at the Mission

Mission life was not always peaceful. There was often discontentment among the Acágchemem living at the mission. They were forced to keep to a strict schedule of classes and work. Converted Indians were only allowed to leave for special reasons like monthly visits to their villages and special harvest times. Many of the Indians living at the mission were resentful of the missionaries' control over their lives.

The Indians' Daily Schedule

▲

The bells at Mission San Juan Capistrano.

At Mission San Juan Capistrano, residents awoke to the sound of the mission bells. The bells rang at dawn telling them to assemble and head to church for Mass, prayers, and lessons. After their religious duties, the neophytes were served a breakfast of *atole*, a mush containing corn or grain.

Following the morning meal, the missionaries gave out work assignments to the Acágchemem men and women. In addition to cooking and tending to the children, the women made baskets in the Acágchemem tradition. The Spanish showed them how to make soap and candles. The Spanish also instructed the women in weaving fabric using looms to make Spanish-style clothes for the men, children, missionaries, soldiers, and themselves. The Acágchemem women also used this method to craft wool blankets.

The men learned how to raise livestock, including cattle, sheep, horses, mules, and goats. Mission San Juan Capistrano established

The mission church, called "The Jewel of the Missions," was considered the most magnificent in all of California. ▶

▲

The mission had an olive press, used to make olive oil.

eight *ranchos*, or ranches, outside the mission complex. The *ranchos* included corrals, stables, sleeping quarters, and a chapel. The men who worked there were called *vaqueros*, meaning cowboys or ranch hands, and they tended to the animals that grazed on mission lands far away from the complex.

The Spanish also taught the men Spanish agricultural methods. They farmed wheat, barley, corn, and vegetables and planted orchards of peaches, walnuts, figs, red and green grapes, oranges, pears, olives, and date palms. The grapes were used to make wine, and the mission had an olive press to press the olives into olive oil. Olive oil was used as cooking oil, lamp oil, and as an item for trade. The mission also traded wine, soap, cloth, and hides with merchant ships for things like nails, musical instruments, furniture, and glass.

The Acágchemem men were also taught various trades. At Mission San Juan Capistrano, the Spanish taught the Indians tanning so they could make saddles, shoes, and hats. The missionaries

▲

A carreta, or wagon.

32

▲

Indians working at the mission.

brought in blacksmiths from San Diego to show the Indians how to work the forge, a furnace for shaping metal. The men learned how to make wagons, called *carretas*, wagon wheels, locks, and keys.

After the morning work session, the Acágchemem took a break for lunch. They ate *pozole*, a soup made of grain, vegetables, and a little meat, out of earthen jars. Then they took a *siesta*, a time for rest or a nap, and returned to work for a short period in the afternoon.

The day concluded with Mass and an *atole* supper. In the evening, the Indians were required to spend time in prayer, church instruction, and language lessons. Then they had some leisure time to dance, sing, and play games.

On occasion, the Spanish held a *fiesta*, or festival, which broke up the monotony of mission life. *Fiestas* were held in honor of various saints, births, weddings, and important events in church history. The Acágchemem also observed some of their traditional ceremonies. Although these rituals were often frowned upon by the friars, many allowed the ceremonies to occur so the Indians would be content and remain peaceful.

The Missionaries' Daily Life

At the mission, the missionaries were called on to perform many tasks. They taught the Acágchemem about religion, crafts, farming, and ranching. They conducted Catholic services, including Mass, baptisms, marriages, and funerals. They also had to keep the peace between the Indians and the soldiers.

The Spanish government required that the missionaries also keep detailed records of life at the mission, including agricultural productivity and success converting Indians. For example, in 1788, the friars recorded that the mission held 2,500 cattle, 7,000 sheep and goats, and 200 mules and horses. In 1811, the mission's agricultural production included 500,000 pounds (186,620 kg) of wheat, 202,000 pounds (75,394 kg) of corn, 190,000 pounds (70,915 kg) of barley, and 20,000 pounds (7,464 kg) of beans. In 1812, about 1,000 Christian Indians lived at the mission.

After the great stone church was destroyed by an earthquake, the friars moved back to a large room in the friar's quarters which had been used as a chapel in Fray Serra's time. Today it is known ▶ as the Serra Chapel because it is the only building where Frey Serra said Mass that still remains standing.

Hardship at the Mission

Mission San Juan Capistrano and the other Alta California missions experienced many hardships. Some problems were caused by the differences between the Spanish and Indian cultures, while other difficulties were the result of disease, pirate raids, and natural disasters.

Clash of Cultures

The Spanish and the Acágchemem living at Mission San Juan Capistrano often clashed. Some of the Indians grew tired of mission life and wanted to return to their old ways. Sometimes the Indians ran away because they weren't allowed to leave without permission. The Spanish hunted them down and brought them back to the mission. Sometimes converts were sent to round up the missing people. The first time an escapee was caught, he was scolded. After that runaways were often whipped or beaten. Indians were also punished if the Spanish thought they weren't working hard enough, or if they stole something.

The Spanish soldiers were often harsh in their treatment of the Indians. Throughout the mission system in Alta California, there were reports that some Indians were beaten severely and that some even died from these beatings.

Not all Acágchemem wanted to join the mission. They were upset that the Spanish had taken over their land. They didn't want to change their lifestyle or religion, but the Spanish were determined to stay. Indians living near some of the missions revolted on occasion. The Acágchemem at Mission San Juan Capistrano lived fairly peacefully because they were interested in learning skills and crafts. When the Indian revolt at Mission San Diego de Alcalá in 1775 caused a delay

◀ *When an escapee was caught, he was scolded or punished.*

in the founding of Mission San Juan Capistrano, it also caused the Spanish to fear that uprisings could happen again at any time.

Mission life was especially confining for single girls and widows. They lived in dormitories, called *monjeríos*, and were kept separate from the other residents. Their quarters, as well as all mission doors, were locked at night to keep the neophytes in and others out. These women spent much time indoors.

Disease

In 1776, the Spanish settled permanently in the area of San Juan Capistrano. At this time the Acágchemem were exposed to many European diseases they had never had contact with before, such as

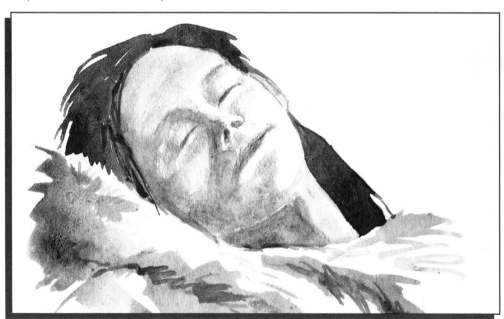

▲
Many of the Indians became ill with or died from European diseases that they had no immunity to.

measles, chickenpox, smallpox, and syphilis. Since the Indians' bodies had not built up any resistance to such diseases, epidemics swept through the missions. Many Indians, 100 in 1806 alone, became very sick and died.

The adobe dormitories also led to much death and disease. They were very cramped and the adobe made the housing cool and damp. The humid air made it hard for some people to breathe, and they became sick. In addition the sanitation systems used by the missionaries attracted bugs and rats carrying germs and disease.

Piracy

In 1818, a group of pirates attacked some of the Alta California missions. These attacks were led by the pirate Hippolyte de Bouchard. The pirates landed near Mission San Juan Capistrano and headed for the mission complex. Fray Gerónimo Boscano learned that the pirates were on their way to attack the mission, so he gathered the Indians and left. No one was left to defend the mission and the large band of pirates stole wine and burned some of the mission buildings.

Natural Disasters

Besides the two years of drought Mission San Juan Capistrano suffered early on, there were other natural disasters that took their toll on the mission. In 1812, just six years after the great stone church was finished, a major earthquake rocked the mission. The disaster occurred in the morning while people were in the church. As the earth began to rumble, the mission bells rang wildly. Many of the Indians were kneeling when the ground began to quake, and they couldn't get out of the church in time. Two boys were in the bell tower to ring the bells for Mass. They were killed when the tower crumbled. The church structure couldn't withstand the force of the earthquake and the heavy roof split and collapsed. In all, 40 people were crushed to death at the mission during the earthquake.

The cloisters at Mission San Juan Capistrano were later damaged by neglect after the mission was abandoned.

Mission San Juan Capistrano's cloisters today.

The earth continued to rumble for a month, causing more damage to the mission buildings. Soon after, floods descended on the land and destroyed crops. The floods, which lasted for one year, caused more damage to the crumbling buildings. Disease plagued the livestock and weeds got into the crop fields.

Secularization and Statehood

In 1810, the people of New Spain started a revolution against the Spanish government in order to gain their independence. During the war, the people living at the missions didn't receive much help from the Spanish government. After 11 years of fighting, the rebels won the war and formed the nation of Mexico. Alta California now belonged to the Mexican government.

The Mexicans had different ideas than the Spanish about how the mission system should operate. Some officials saw the missions as a way to increase their personal wealth. Others thought that the Indians living and working at the missions were being treated like slaves. In August 1834, laws were passed by the Mexican government to secularize the missions. Rather than turn the lands over to the Indians as the Spanish had intended, these laws gave the mission lands, buildings, crops, and livestock to the Mexican government. Most of the land that was supposed to go to the Indians ended up in the hands of local landowners or Mexican officials.

Mission San Juan Capistrano was different, though. Governor José Figueroa chose this mission as the site of a *pueblo de indios*, an Indian city with a municipal government. The mission buildings were converted into city administration buildings. The daily operations of the mission were turned over to the converted Acágchemem to run. However, a Mexican official was placed in charge of the overall operation.

Within the first couple of years, the *pueblo de indios* collapsed. The Acágchemem complained to Governor Figueroa that the official in charge was using their labor for his own personal gain. They also reported that he illegally sold off a lot of the land, as well as the livestock and several buildings, to settlers. As a result, many of the Indians left the *pueblo* and

Mission San Juan Capistrano went through many changes when it became secularized. ▶

took jobs in Los Angeles as *vaqueros*, cooks, or factory workers. By 1840, there were only about 100 Indians living at the mission.

In the 1840s, Americans began settling in California and petitioned the United States government to make California a state. American troops fought the Mexicans for control of the land, and won the war with Mexico(1846–1848).

Many of the Indians left the pueblo and took jobs in Los Angeles.

President Abraham Lincoln returned Mission San Juan Capistrano to the church.

Gold was discovered shortly after the the war. In 1850, California became the 31st state. In 1865, President Abraham Lincoln signed the order returning Mission San Juan Capistrano to the Catholics.

45

The Legacy of Mission San Juan Capistrano

By the 1860s, Mission San Juan Capistrano was in ruins. Its buildings were plundered. The bricks, tiles, and wood that once made up the walls and roofs at the mission were stolen by local settlers who used the materials to build their homes and businesses. For the next 30 years, the mission continued to crumble.

However, the town around the mission grew rapidly. The California Central Railroad was built in 1887, and San Juan Capistrano was the halfway point between San Diego and Los Angeles. Local farmers could easily transport their crops of oranges, walnuts, barley, and olives to large cities using the train. By the beginning of the twentieth century, the town was thriving.

In 1895, the Landmarks Club of California started an effort to restore the mission. They raised money to purchase supplies and did some work. In 1910, Father John O'Sullivan of the mission church began restoration of the mission. The work was publicized in the *Los Angeles Times*. This drew the attention of the Hollywood crowd. In 1939, Leon René composed the hit song "When the Swallows Come Back to Capistrano." By the 1940s, the mission had become a popular tourist spot.

The great stone church of Mission San Juan Capistrano undergoing restoration.

Today Mission San Juan Capistrano is still undergoing restoration. Many of the workshops, factories, kitchens, and living quarters appear as they did in the late 1700s and early 1800s. The chapel looks

◀ *Visitors sit inside the quadrangle of Mission San Juan Capistrano.*

much the way it did when Fray Serra conducted religious services there more than 200 years ago.

Mission San Juan Capistrano is an important historical site. Ten acres (4.06 hectares) of the original mission complex have been turned into an outdoor museum illustrating the lifestyle of the Spanish missionaries and the Acágchemem who lived at the mission. The center offers educational classes about California's history to school groups.

▲

Mission San Juan Capistrano's central courtyard.

Visitors to the center can tour the grounds and restored buildings. They can peek into a *kiitca* like those the Acágchemem lived in before the Spanish arrived, or they can see the factories where the mission workers made candles, soap, olive oil, and wine. Other things to see at the center include the original mission bells, cemetery, Serra Chapel, soldiers' barracks, jail, and the ruins of the great stone church destroyed in the earthquake of 1812.

The center contains exhibits on tools, baskets, winemaking,

The mission cemetery.

◀ *This fountain is in the center of the mission.*

▲
This is a replica of an Acágchemem home.

49

A view of Mission San Juan Capistrano surrounded by rich plant life.

plants and herbs, and the swallows that build their nests on the mission grounds.

The influences the missions had on the state of California are evident today. Farming and ranching techniques first taught by the Spanish friars are now a major part of California's industry. Many of the crops begun at the missions, such as olives, grapes, and oranges, are still produced. The work that was done by the missionaries and Indians more than 200 years ago has made California one of the leading agricultural centers in the United States.

This monument, erected in 1924 to honor the Acágchemem Indians, reads: "In this holy place lie the bodies of those who built the mission. May their souls rest in peace." ▶

IN THIS HOLY PLACE LIE THE
BODIES OF THOSE WHO BUILT
THE MISSION · MAY THEIR SOULS
REST IN PEACE · ERECTED 19__

Make Your Own Model
Mission San Juan Capistrano

To make your own model of the San Juan Capistrano mission, you will need:

X-Acto knife (ask an adult for help)
ruler
foamcore
glue
tape
pencil
modeling clay

toothpicks
bells
cream- and green-colored paint
red felt
cardboard
colored construction or tissue paper

Directions

Step 1: To make the base, cut a foamcore rectangle that measures 20" x 15" (50.8 x 38.1 cm). Paint with green paint. Let dry.

Step 2: To make the workshops, cut a foamcore rectangle that measures 17" x 2.5" (43.1 x 6.4 cm).

2.5" (6.4 cm)

17" (43.1 cm)

Adult supervision is suggested.

Step 3: Take one of the rectangles. Draw a faint line with pencil 7" (17.8 cm) from the edge. Bend the board along this line.

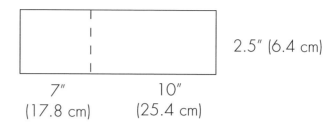

2.5" (6.4 cm)

7" (17.8 cm)   10" (25.4 cm)

Step 4: Cut a 13" x 2" (33 x 5.1 cm) piece. Cut arches in the bottom. Draw a line 5" (12.7 cm) from edge. Bend the board along this line.

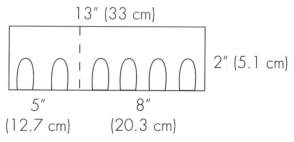

13" (33 cm)

2" (5.1 cm)

5" (12.7 cm)   8" (20.3 cm)

Step 5: To make the sides of the workshop, cut two 2" x 3.5" (5.1 x 8.9 cm) house-shaped pieces.

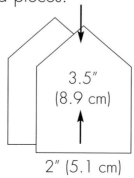

3.5" (8.9 cm)

2" (5.1 cm)

Step 6: Glue together front, back, and side walls to make an "L" shape. Attach to base.

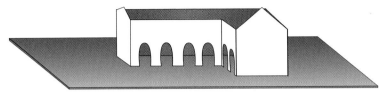

Step 7: To make the church, cut a 17" x 14" (43.2 x 35.6 cm) foamcore rectangle. Cut a 5" x 5" (12.7 x 12.7 cm) square out of each corner, leaving a plus sign.

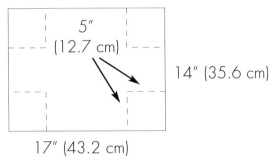

5"
(12.7 cm)

14" (35.6 cm)

17" (43.2 cm)

Step 8: Fold the sides of the plus sign up to form a box. Tape sides on the inside of the box shape.

Step 9: Turn the box shape over and attach to base.

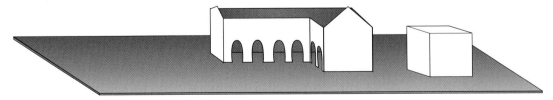

Step 10: To make the tower, make a 9" x 9" (22.9 x 22.9 cm) square and a 4.5" x 4.5" (11.4 x 11.4 cm) square. Cut four 3" (7.6 cm) corners out of the larger square. Cut four 1.5" (3.8 cm) corners out of the smaller square. Repeat the folding instructions followed for the church. Add a ball of clay to the top of the tower. Stick a toothpick cross in the clay ball.

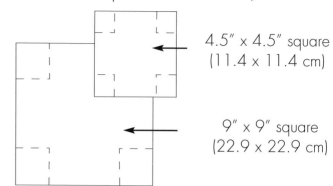

4.5" x 4.5" square
(11.4 x 11.4 cm)

9" x 9" square
(22.9 x 22.9 cm)

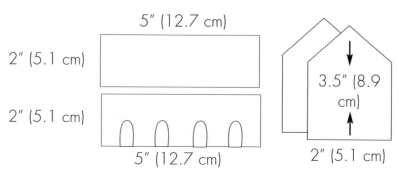

Step 11: To make the soldier's quarters, cut out two 5" x 2" (12.7 x 5.1 cm) pieces and two 2" x 3.5" (5.1 x 8.9 cm) pieces with triangular house tops from the foamcore. Cut doors from one 5" x 2" (12.7 x 5.1 cm) piece.

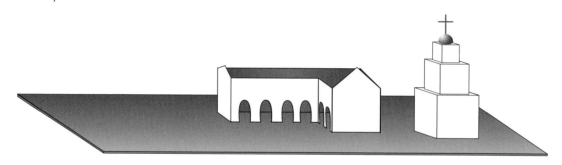

5" (12.7 cm)

2" (5.1 cm)

2" (5.1 cm)

5" (12.7 cm)

3.5" (8.9 cm)

2" (5.1 cm)

55

Step 12: Glue together pieces to make a house. To make the friars' quarters and the kitchen, repeat steps for making soldiers' quarters.

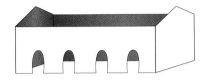

Step 13: Cut out a 4" x 2" (10.2 x 5.1 cm) piece to make the bell wall. Cut out holes for bells and glue bells in place.

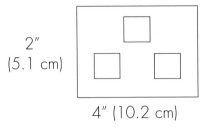

2"
(5.1 cm)

4" (10.2 cm)

Step 14: Place the buildings on the base and paint them cream. For the workshops' roofs, cut out a 7" x 3.75" (17.8 x 9.5 cm), and an 8" x 3.75" (20.3 x 9.5 cm) piece of foamcore, bend each rectangle in half the long way.

3.75" (9.5 cm)

3.75" (9.5 cm)

8" (20.3 cm)

7" (17.8 cm)

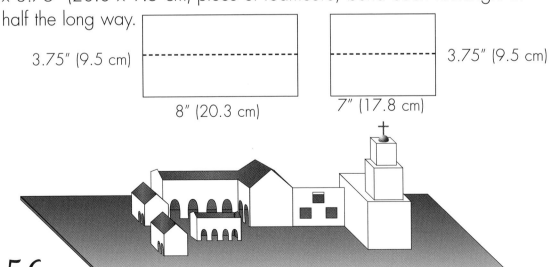

Step 15: Cut out three 5" x 3.75" (12.7 x 9.5 cm) rectangles for the roofs of the soldiers' quarters, friars' quarters, and kitchen. Fold them in half.

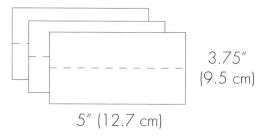

3.75"
(9.5 cm)

5" (12.7 cm)

Step 16: Attach roofs to the buildings and cover with red felt. Decorate the mission with flowers and trees which you can make out of colored construction or tissue paper. Add a cross to the top of the bell tower. You can make the cross out of toothpicks and a small ＋ ball of clay.

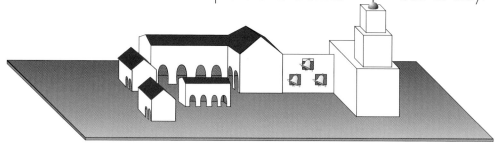

*Use the above mission as a reference for building your mission.

Important Dates in Mission History

1492	Christopher Columbus reaches the West Indies
1542	Cabrillo's expedition to California
1602	Sebastián Vizcaíno sails to California
1713	Fray Junípero Serra is born
1769	Founding of San Diego de Alcalá
1770	Founding of San Carlos Borromeo del Río Carmelo
1771	Founding of San Antonio de Padua and San Gabriel Arcángel
1772	Founding of San Luis Obispo de Tolosa
1775–76	**Founding of San Juan Capistrano**
1776	Founding of San Francisco de Asís
1776	Declaration of Independence is signed
1777	Founding of Santa Clara de Asís
1782	Founding of San Buenaventura
1784	Fray Serra dies
1786	Founding of Santa Bárbara
1787	Founding of La Purísima Concepción
1791	Founding of Santa Cruz and Nuestra Señora de la Soledad
1797	Founding of San José, San Juan Bautista, San Miguel Arcángel, and San Fernando Rey de España
1798	Founding of San Luis Rey de Francia
1804	Founding of Santa Inés
1817	Founding of San Rafael Arcángel
1823	Founding of San Francisco de Solano
1848	Gold found in northern California
1850	California becomes the 31st state

Glossary

adobe (uh-DOH-bee) Sun-dried bricks made of straw, mud, and sometimes manure.

Alta California (AL-tuh ka-luh-FOR-nyuh) The area where the Spanish settled missions, today known as the state of California.

Baja California (BAH-ha ka-luh-FOR-nyuh) The Mexican peninsula directly south of the state of California.

baptize (BAP-tyz) To perform the ceremony that accepts someone into the Christian faith.

cathedral (kuh-THEE-druhl) A large church built in the shape of a cross.

Christian (KRIS-chun) Someone who follows the Christian religion, or the teachings of Jesus Christ and the Bible.

convert (kun-VERT) To change religious beliefs.

Franciscan (fran-SIS-kin) A communal Roman Catholic order of friars, or "brothers" who follow the teachings and examples of Saint Francis of Assisi who did much work as a missionary.

friar (FRY-ur) A brother in a communal religious order. Friars can also be priests.

granary (GRAY-nuh-ree) A place to store grain.

lash (LASH) To tie or fasten together with a rope.

missionary (MIH-shun-ayr-ee) A person who teaches his or her religion to people with different beliefs.

neophyte (NEE-oh-fyt) The name for American Indians baptized into the Christian faith.

New Spain (NOO SPAYN) The area where the Spanish colonists had their capital in North America, and that would later become Mexico.

plunder (PLUHN-der) To rob.

quadrangle (KWAH-drayn-gul) The square at the center of a mission that is surrounded by four buildings.

ritual (RIH-choo-uhl) A ceremony marking an event.

secularization (sehk-yoo-luh-rih-ZAY-shun) A process by which the mission lands were made to be nonreligious.

tanning (TA-ning) Making animal hides into leather by soaking them in a special liquid.

60

Pronunciation Guide

atole (ah-TOH-lay)

carretas (kah-RAY-tahs)

fiestas (fee-EHS-tahs)

fray (FRAY)

kiitcas (KEE-shas)

monjerío (mohn-hay-REE-oh)

pozole (poh-SOH-lay)

pueblo de indios (PWAY-bloh DAY IN-dee-ohs)

ranchos (RAHN-chohs)

siesta (see-EHS-tah)

tejas (TAY-hahs)

terrado (teh-RAH-doh)

vaqueros (bah-KEH-rohs)

Resources

For more information about Mission San Juan Capistrano and the California Missions, check out these books and Web sites:

Books:

Lyngheim, Linda. *The Indians and the California Missions.* Van Nuys, CA: Langtry Publications, 1990.

Palóu, Francisco. *The Founding of the First California Missions.* San Francisco: Nueva California Press, 1934.

Web Sites:

History of San Juan Capistrano
http://www.sanjuancapistrano.org/history.html

Mission San Juan Capistrano Cultural Center
http://www.missionsjc.com/

Index